THE TALES OF MAHARANA PRATAP

THE GREAT RAJPUT WARRIOR

ABHIGYA SINGH RAJAWAT

DEDICATION

A very special thanks to my Dad, Mukesh Bahadur Singh, for helping me publish this book. He was always willing to help me with this. I must say I couldn't have done any of this without him. I wrote this book myself. I could thank here today. I also thank my mother, Rishika Singh for always beliving in me and giving me just the advice I needed. She helped me accomplish this goal.

Contents

Preface

PREFACE

One day I thought about Freedom Fighters and decided to make a project on them but then I got this thought. Why not about a king or somebody like that. My first and last thought was Maharana Pratap. My dad then gave me an intresting idea. He said "How about you write a book on Maharana Pratap?" which seemed really intresting and I must say, it truly was.

CHAPTER ONE

FAMILY

Pratap sure had lots of Family members and it could be confusing to read the book without properly knowing them all. So here, all of them listed-

Grandfather- Rana Sangram Singh/ Rana Sanga.

Grandmother- Rani Karnavati/ Rani Karmavati

Father- King Udai Singh

Mothers-

1. [Biological mother] Maharani Jaiwanta Bai

2. [Second oldest] Rani Dheer Bai

3. [Third oldest mother] Rani Sajja Baina

4. [Youngest mother] Rani Veer Bai

Brothers-

1. Kunwar Shakti Singh

2. Kunwar Vikramdev Singh

3. Kunwar Jagmal Singh

4. Sagar Singh

Sisters [stepsisters]-

1. Chand Kanwar

2. Man Kanwar

Wives-

1. [First, favourite wife] Ajabde Punwar

2. Phool Bai Rathore

3. Alamdebai Chauhan

4. Amarbai Rathore

5. Ratnawatibai Parmar

6. Jasobai Chauhan

7. Champabai Jhati

8. Lakhabai

9. Kichar Asha bai

10. Solankhinipur Bai

11. Shahmatibai Hada

Sons-

1. Amar Singh- Maharani Ajabde

2. Kunwar Durjan Singh- Rani Champabai

3. Kunwar Maal Singh- Rani Ratnawati bai

4. Shekha Singh/Shekhar Singh- Rani Phoolbai

5. Kunwar Ram Singh- Rani Kichar Asha bai

6. Kunwar Raibhana Singh- Rani Lakhabai

7. Chanda Singh- Rani Phoolbai

8. Kunwar Hathi Singh- Rani Kichar Asha bai

9. Kunwar Natha Singh- Rani Amarbai

10. Kunwar Kalyan Das- Rani Jasobai

11. Sahas Mal- Rani Solankhinpur bai

12. Kunwar Jaswant Singh- Rani Alamdebai

13. Kunwar Puran Mal- Rani Shahmatibai

14. Kunwar Gopal- Rani Solankhinpur bai

15. Kunwar Sanwal Das Singh- Rani Champabai

16. Bhagwan Das- Maharani Ajabde

17. Kunwar Kachra Singh- Rani Champabai

Daughters-

[5 names are unknown]

Grandsons-

1. Kunwar Karan Singh- Amar Singh

2. Kunwar Sujarmal- Amar Singh

CHAPTER TWO

LOSING THE WAR OF HALDIGHATI

Maharana Pratap certainly loved his life in Chittorgarh even though he spent his whole childhood in the Kumbalgarh castle. But the actual reason that King Udai and his family moved to Chittor was because Akbar was quicky taking over and Kumbalgarh was no longer that safe now. Pratap had spent most of his life in Chittor and dearly enjoyed it there. He even became King there at the age of 32. But sadly, after losing the war of Haldighati he also lost Chittor. Akbar was sure that Pratap would do anything to win Chittor back and it was true. But since they had lost Chittor, they had nowhere to go. Fortunately a forest tribe, the Bhils, took them in. After this, with only 22,000 men left while Akbar had 80,000, Pratap tried the Guerilla Warfare technique. They used to attack in small groups one after another. This way they saved much more men. But for how long would Maharana Pratap, his family and soldiers stay in the forest? It was already tough there. So after this a bit in the south of Chittor, brick-by-brick, passing them he, his people and the Bhils built a new city, Udaipur, which Pratap named after his father in his honour. Sadly soon after, King

Udai peacefully came to an end, which unforunately, brought everyone's confidence and courage down, even Maharana Pratap's.

Maharana Pratap spent the rest of life trying to win back Chittor from the Mughal rule but could never suceed in that. But later, in 1615, King Amar singh, Maharana Pratap's son, won back the fort after signing a treaty with Shah Jahn, Akbar's decsandant. As tribute to him, near the Gandhi sagar, which is in the south of Udaipur, there is also a Rana Pratap Sagar and a Rana Pratap Dam.

CHAPTER THREE

His Trustworthy Horse

Almost 600 years ago, there were only 3 major breeds of horses and they were Marwadi, Sindi and Kathiawadi. Chetak, was a Marwadi horse. He had a muscular lean body, a body with a high forehead with sparkling eyes and a long face. These were the qualities that made him look different than any other horse. But there is diffrence of opinion amongst historians about what breed Chetak was? He is mostly said to be Marwari horse only, but some say he was a Kathiwadi horse. The first folk tale states him as a Kathiwadi horse.

There are many popular stories that describe how Maharana Pratap and Chetak met but the two most famous ones are-

The first folk tale is- One day the Danti Charan traders from Surendranagar district in Kathiwar presented two Kathiwadi horses, from which one was Chetak, to Maharana Pratap. He saw the horse in his eyes and saw his spirit deep inside and said " I like this one."

The second folk tale is- One day Maharana Pratap decided to go to the market with his beloved wife, Ajabde and of course they went under disguise. But even as they walked Pratap kept looking around, checking for any danger. Suddenly he heard some commotion. Both walked there. It was a horse market and there were competitions going around so everyone could see for themselves how strong the horses truly are and surely, they were. Soon came out a white stealthy-looking horse and indeed it was Chetak. Pratap saw and suddenly became intrested. He saw how free and wild the horse was, how it wasn't afraid of anything. Nothing or nobody dared to step into his way. Then came out the riding competition. In this people could volunteer to ride any horse that was competing and see if the horse suited them. But everyone who tried to get on Chetak fell and got hurt. Then Pratap raised his hand and said " I would like to try and ride this white horse." And sure enough he rode Chetak without any hesitation, astonishing everone who was there to witness it. The host said " Oh sir, what can I say, nobody else can ride him but you. You may take him for free. " No sir, It is your horse and I cannot just take him without paying. I will buy him but please, do tell me his name?" said Pratap kindly. " He is Chetak." Said the host and soon after paying, Pratap Ajabde and Chetak set off for the palace.

CHAPTER FOUR

MEANING OF JOHAR?

One midnight young Pratap went to his mother. Seeing him awake his mother Jaiwanta bai told him to sleep. Pratap quietly came and lay down on Jaiwanta bai's lap. After a while or two Rana Uday entered the room and saw Pratap sleeping but Pratap was actually pretending. He was awake but closed his eyes as soon as he saw his mother talking to Rana Uday. She asked him "what happened, you look worried? ". Rana Uday said "Enemies are almost at the door and in the least case if we are unable to stop them, johar might have to be done. Jaiwanta bai was horrified but bravely said " I desprately wish that it doesn't, but I'll get the johar room cleansed tomorrow. Pratap overheard this and was confused but decided to find out what was Johar.

The next day he hid in an enormus drum about to be carried in the Johar room. Soon he felt that the drum, he was sitting in was being carried, he peeked out.

said' Pratap, please come out of the drum, staying there a long time is not good for your health. Pratap thought that his mother would scold him, came out of the drum. It was a dark room with each corner either covered with dirt or spiderwebs. Jaiwanta bai however was not angry and said, "Pratap, men are not allowed to come here". Pratap felt ashamed a bit and said, mother please, can you tell me what is Johar? Jaiwanta bai said, Ohh Pratap, who told you about Johar? Pratap said ashamed , I heard you and father overtalk yesterday night. Jaiwanta said Johar is not important but still it is time for you to know the meaning of it. Pratap agreed and listened carefully. Jaiwanta bai then told him but along his mother's words, Pratap started to imagine all that.

He found himself in the same room but this time it was very clean and covered in flowers and brightness. There was a large place in the middle of the room that looked like a hole. Many women began to fill the room along with his grandmother and lots more. There were dasis holding plates full of Kum-Kum. Soon his grandmother, queen Karnavati/Karmavati, put her hand flat on one of them. Her hands became red and she walked towards the walls. She imprinted her hands on each wall and one by one the other women started following her. After some time all the walls were stained with the hand imprints of each woman who was there. Then the dasis began to throw huge logs of wood in the enormous hole. Then they lit the wood on fire. One of the women said'' Oh maharani ji. Will we have to do this?''. The queen said '' Oh Padmavati, I wish not but yes, everybody has to.'' All the women became sad. '' Huh? Why are you all so sad? We are the women of this kingdom. We are strong and can die fighting, can't we? If our husbands can go out happily in the battlefield to die for the kingdom then why can't we? We should be grateful that we got to die for our people.'' Everybody nodded and chanted '' Jai Mewar! Jai maharani ji ki! Jai Mewar! Pratap was confused. What were they going to do? Then finally they said '' Jai Mewar!'' and all of them jumped into the fire!

Pratap was shocked and baffled. Suddenly he felt a hand on his shoulder. " Pratap, are you alright?!" everything came back to normal and his mother said " I knew this was a bad idea. You should go now Pratap. It is not good for you to stay here any longer." and so Pratap said " I won't let that happen to you! I will fight. Nobody will have to do Johar! Not as long as I am there".

CHAPTER FIVE

THE PERFECT TEACHER

One day in the palace, Kunwar Shakti and Kunwar Vikram[Pratap's younger brothers] challenged Pratap to come and play hide and and seek with them in the caves not far away but they said this making weird faces. '' No, I am sorry but you know that we are not allowed to go there.'' said responsible Pratap. Shakti in a rude tone now said '' Huh! Looks like to me that you are just scared of the dark scary big caves. But don't worry, you can have your friend Dudda or whatever he is of yours.'' which triggered Pratap's anger. ''Fine whatever. I'll call Dudda, and he is my friend.'' Soon all 4 of the kids reached the cave and entred. Shakti started the game and said '' There will be two teams, Me and Vikram will be the first one and bhayiya [Pratap] and Dudda will be the second one. We will set of different paths and whoever finds the other one first, wins. 3,2,1 GO!!! and off they went. But soon they met, stuck behind athe same wall. Pratap, Dudda, Shakti and Vikram pushed with all their might but could not fully suceed, they could only move it a littlle bit of it. Dudda was getting nervous and fainted. Pratap got panicked and in his stress he by mistake almost broke the wall. He quickly got Dudda out too and thought " I need water to wake Dudda but were will I find it ? Suddenly he thought " Ofcourse! I can try and break the sidewalls incase there are any water channels in there. He took his dagger out and started to poke the wall with it. " What are you doing?!" said a voice, very angry. "Who said that?! Show yourself if you aren't a coward." said shocked Pratap. Suddenly a man came running, wearing a white shawl-like-cloth as if he were a learned guru but Pratap didn't recognise this at first. He shouted " Don't ever do that again unless you want to face my wrath!". "Can't you see that my friend is unconcious? All I did was try to get some water for him!" said Pratap becoming red." You, proud prince, have disgraced this holy cave! Here take this bottle, and go away, and don't ever try and come here again." said the guru looking as if he were about to burst with anger. Pratap took Dudda and the bottle and said to Shakti and Vikram, " Come, we are going back to the palace you two". Pratap, after reaching the palace in afternoon, was left wordless. He was very intrigued to learn more from the wise guru that he met in the cave. He thought " That guru really was very learned, I must try and search for him to see if he accepts me as his student...". Immediatly, Rana Uday Singh walked into the room and asked, " What happned Pratap, why in such deep thought? How about this, we have lunch, and you can tell me more about it." Pratap said " Sure father, why not?" and thus, father and son went through in to the dining room. Pratap said everything truthfully and his dad said" Pratap, I am pleased to hear that you feel so and even more to see that you want to be such a wise guru's student. How about we go to his ashram and talk to him about this?" Pratap replied "All right, lets." Thus both went to the forest behing the hills with a few soldiers. After a difficult test Pratap had a new guru, the wisest he'd met till now.

CHAPTER SIX

GOD'S FLOWER

One day Jaiwanta Bai was about to perform a puja for lord Vishnu. She thought '' Let me call Pratap also''. Saying so the rani called her dasis and said '' Phoolvati , please call Pratap for this special puja. Phoolvati [The dasi] who was already very nervous, and was about to step out of the room replied " But your majesty Kuwar Pratap is not even in the palace" '' He went away to the Vishnu pond but he does not know it had ccc-c... -CROCODILES!!! Meanwhile, Pratap, by the time, had already reached the Vishnu Pond. He saw an extremely exquisite flower. He knew that it was the Rare Vishnu lotus flower. But there were crocodiles swimming round and round encircling the rare flower! Pratap thought of a plan and climbed a tree which was near the pond. Then he clung to a branch and Alas! Pratap was just about to fall when he put his foot on another branch and carefully tried to reach the flower. But soon one of the crocodiles saw him and tried to catch Pratp's arm with his razor sharp teeth. " Ahh, Oh just a bit more!" said Pratap and after a little amount of tries reached the flower just in time! Pratap said" ahhaa! Yes! I got the perfect Vishnu flower!" and got off the tree. "Baoji Raj! Baoji Raj!" said Dudda[Pratap's best friend]. " Yes Dudda! I am here!". Panting,Huffing and puffing Dudda ran over to Pratap and said " Oh! So you are here Baoji Raj! Maharani Jaiwanta bai is calling you for the Vishnu Puja. Lets go!" Pratap said "Ohh! Yes! Lets go!" saying so, the 2 boys ran till the Mewar Qila. Pratap ran through the corridor, into the dining room and finally found the mandir and said " Ranimaa, I have got the beautiful and rare Vishnu lotus flower, just for you!"

CHAPTER SEVEN

AKBAR AND PRATAP FRIENDS?

One day to find the Mughal Emperor Akbar and Pratap set out on a new journey. He disguised himself as a farmer and went into the village. After half way Pratap felt hungry and stopped near a temple where food was going to be served for free. Another boy of Pratap's age was also there. Actually that boy was Akbar looking for Pratap but both of them did not know this. Soon sworn enemies started to become friends and they met each other everyday at the village still with hope to find who they were looking for. One day while returning home Akbar told his painter to make Pratap's portrait by telling him how to make him as a gift for Pratap. Pratap was doing the same thing. Soon Pratap's mother came there and as soon as she saw the portrait she was horrified and said in anger' Ohhh Pratap, who is this ? Pratap said it was his friend. Akbar's mother asked the same question but Akbar also said he was his friend. Soon Jaiwanta bai and Akbar's mother told them whom they were friends with. Pratap and Akbar were very angry at each other and thought " How could he betray me? We were so close and were good friends but all of it was probably just a trap to make me trust him so one day when he has the oppurtunity he would have killed me quietly! I shall never meet him again!

A NEW BROTHER FOR PRATAP

Rani Dheerbai [Pratap's stepmother] was pregnant and Rana Uday took good care of Rani Dheerbai.Pratap was also very very excited to meet his new brother.One day which actually was the day predicted for Rani Dheerbai to deliver a healthy baby boy Pratap went to gurukul and by half of the time of the gurukul Pratap thought that'Has my small baby brother arrived in this world meanwhile a royal soldier came to gurukul and said ' Is prince Pratap here? Pratap's guru, Acharya Raghavendra ji, said' Yes,Pratap is here. Can you give this scroll to him?It is from the king, said the soldier handing him a long scroll. Acharya ji took it and gave it to Pratap.The scroll said' Oh dear Pratap, you were my only child till now with your brother Shakti and Vikram. Yet today you have another brother. Yes, Rani Dheerbai is no longer pregnant and has given birth to a boy. Now I have 4 young princes, filling the palace with the joy and happiness it has needed for a while now. Please come and bring your brothers too."Pratap was very happy and said with hope' Master my brother finally has arrived in this world and I can't wait to meet him. Can I go now please?

His master sighed and said 'Yes you can go to the palace and meet your newborn brother but come back soon. Pratap very happy ran to the palace as fast as he could and went to Dheerbai's room and saw her sleeping with her baby[Pratap's new brother]and saw his father also sitting next to Dheerbai holding her hand.And Pratap named his newborn brother' Jagmal' [The one who rules the world].

CHAPTER NINE

FOOD POISNER

" I want him killed!" Shouted Emperor Akbar." Every time I hire someone to kill that, that, that Pratap he always escapes! How? how?" Then Mahamanga , [Akbar's close Nanny] said " Emperor Akbar, If you would allow then may I share something? " Fine. You may." said Akbar. " Thank you my lord, what I wanted to say is that I have thought of a plan to finish Pratap." Akbar said " Yes, I am listening." " I have hired Gauherjan, a serial killer. She has never failed till today and I think she can kill Pratap." " But how can we trust her ammi jan[a way to say nanny/mother in mughals different language]? " asked Akbar. Mahamanga said " Oh, don't worry about that my dear emperor .Gauherjan is trustable till we pay her handsomely." Akbar said " Fine, ammi jan, I suppose you can recruit and then send Gauherjan." So, Gauherjan went to bijolia[A state included in Mewar where Pratap currently was]on her horse. Bijolia's king, Rao Mamrak ji had a daughter, Ajabde. Ajabde had a friend, the princess of marwar named Phool Kanwar. Phool Kawar was also at Bijolia and had started dance classes with ' Laal Bai ' Her new teacher. However, Gauherjan made her way to Laal Bai's cart to kill her and Disguise herself as Laal Bai and succeeded in it. Then by the next morning, she reached Bijolia's castle and told Rao Mamrak ji that she was Laal Bai, Phool Kawar's new dance teacher. Happy, he invited her in the palace and introduced her to Phool Kawar. Then later, when Pratap had gone to check the borders for any enimies that may have lurking around there, trying to devise any strategies to attack Mewar or Bijolia, Phool Kawar had to make the food and called Laal Bai and Ajabde to help her with it.But secretly, Gauherjan mixed poison in the food which was going to Pratap's camp! Later, when Ajabde asked how much sugar she had put in the kheer, Phool said " Don't worry, I put lots of sugar from the bag kept on the right shelves." Ajabde then screamed " What!? Did you say the sugar from the right shelves!? " Yes" said Phool" No Phool no, the sugar that was kept on the right shelves was not sugar! It was salt! Expired salt!" Phool then said " Oh no, Ajabde! You have to help me to make the food again or else Kuwar Pratap might get sick because of the expired salt!" ." Come!we need to go, quickly! We have to make new food and replace it with the bad one. Come!" "Yes, said Ajabde, lets go." And so after a while the two girls had made fresh food and ran to Pratap's camp. There they saw that Pratap was already about to take a bite when there came a voice from inside the jungle! Pratap heard it and immediately ran over there. His friends also ran behind Pratap. As soon as Pratap and his friends ran to the jungle, Ajabde and Phool Kawar quickly went and changed the bad food with the fresh one. And Gauherjan on the other hand, decided to go and look with her own eyes to see Pratap die! She hurried through the jungle. Later after helping the person, Pratap and his friends came back and ate the food heartily. " What!?" thought Gauherjan angrily . " Bu-Bu-,But how! I mixed poison in it! How are they still alive!?" " Urghh! PRATAP!!"

21

The End

THANK YOU FOR READING THIS BOOK

If you enjoyed reading this book then stay tuned for my next one! Our country India has a very rich culture and art and to know more about it, you can definetly do a bit of research!

Bye!!!